Forgiving

Is Smart for Your Heart

Written by
Carol Ann Morrow

Illustrated by
R. W. Alley

ONE
CARING
PLACE

Abbey Press
St. Meinrad, IN 47577

For Pat Barker,
who believes forgiveness
is the most important lesson
and teaches that lesson so well.

Text © 2003 Carol Ann Morrow
Illustrations © 2003 St. Meinrad Archabbey
Published by One Caring Place
Abbey Press
St. Meinrad, Indiana 47577

Library of Congress Catalog Number
2002111572

ISBN 978-0-87029-370-2

Printed in the United States of America

A Message to Parents, Teachers, and Other Caring Adults

We've all heard the expression "Forgive and forget." The real order of the universe, however, is "Remember and forgive." The purpose of this book is to help you guide your children in that true order. This does not mean allowing and accepting injustice, injury, or abuse. Adults as well as children need to name, recognize, and challenge these. Forgiveness goes a step further. It is letting go of any need to "get even." It is believing that every person is more than any single action—even actions that seem to cause pain and sadness.

Children are very forgiving by nature. They continue along this path, unless we teach them something else. And we do teach them in many ways— most of them not verbal. We may teach them to hold grudges, when they see us withhold our love. We teach them volumes through what we reveal in our words of complaint, our words of anger. We teach them by our gestures, our postures, our attitudes. Who needs words?

Yet I dare to offer some. Psychologist William Damon, author of *The Moral Child,* encourages caring adults to nurture children's moral growth—as surely as we nurture their growing bodies with food and drink and exercise. Dr. Damon says that caring adults have four steps to take in fostering moral virtue. I've applied the steps he's described to encouraging a spirit of forgiveness.

First, support and nurture the child's innate forgiving nature. Second, help the child see and name situations in which forgiveness is—or could be— expressed. Third, encourage forgiving words and actions. Lastly, challenge any lack of forgiveness by creating chances for a change of heart. No festering, only fostering!

You and I experience forgiveness every day in a very physical way. We experience a body renewed after a night's rest. Daily, we and the earth are given a new chance with the sunrise. As in our bodies and on our earth, forgiveness can be in our hearts—and in our children's hearts. Forgiving is smart for your heart.

—*Carol Ann Morrow*

Your Heart Is Smart

Some days have bumps in them. You can get a bump on your knee or on your heart.

Theresa broke Sarah's new pencil. Theresa says she didn't mean to, but Sarah feels sad. James didn't pick Ben for the team. Ben is mad at James.

Sarah and Ben could hold on to their hurt feelings. They could stay sad or mad. But they could also make another choice. They could let go. They could forgive.

Forgiving is good for happy living. Your heart knows how to forgive. When you do it over and over, you get even better at it.

To Forgive Is to Give

The word *give* is inside the word *forgive*. Giving and forgiving are a lot alike. When you say, "It's okay," to Jasmine, you are giving her a gift. That gift is letting go of what she did or said. You give away your reason to be mad or hurt.

Forgiving is like erasing a chalkboard. Some teachers write your name on the board when you get in trouble. When your name is gone, everything is all right again. You can erase Jasmine's name from your blackboard by forgiving her.

Forgiving does not mean that nothing happened. You know you could make Jasmine feel bad for what she did. But you want to help her to feel good and be good. You want to give her a new chance.

Forgiving Opens Your Heart

Maybe your mom said she would take you to the circus, but she forgot. Or your uncle said he would bring you a present, but he doesn't have one.

You could be sad and quiet. You could pitch a fit or be mean. You might not talk or be friendly.

Hurting people who hurt you may seem fair. But it really just keeps the hurt going. It traps both of you inside a dark cloud of bad feelings. Forgiving opens your heart, so you can let out the hurt and let love shine in.

How to Forgive

To show forgiveness, you might say: "I'm okay. It's okay." "I know you didn't mean it." "You're my friend. I'll let it pass." " I love you."

Don't say: "It doesn't matter," when it really does. Or, "Forget it," if you wish someone would remember to act another way.

You can also show forgiveness by your actions. Look your friend in the eye and smile or shake hands. Hug your dad or sit close to your mom. Do something extra nice. Don't wait too long, so the person knows this is about forgiving.

What Does Forgiving Look Like?

There are many different ways to forgive. Let's say your little brother keeps taking your ball away. You can play with him for a while to show him how to share and play together.

Maybe your dad said he would go to the park with you. Now he says he's too tired. You can tell him, "I like to be with you. You rest now and we can go tomorrow."

Carrie tries to sneak ahead in the lunch line. You let Carrie know in a kind way that she isn't being fair or polite: "Carrie, get in line next to me. We can get there at almost the same time."

Holding On to Hurt Is Hard— on You!

If you choose not to forgive, your hurt holds on—with claws, like a frightened kitty. It hurts. It grows. It weighs you down.

You may think you are "getting back" at the person who hurt you by being mad, but he may not even know what you're thinking. He may be happy while you aren't. How is that helping you? How are you helping anyone?

You can decide to let go of your mad feelings. You can wish the other person well. You can pray for him. You can show him, by your own good choices, how to be a good person.

Forgiving Is Freeing

When you forgive, you don't pretend that nothing happened. You really did want Alexis to invite you to her party. You wanted the coach to let you play.

But you decide to forgive. You choose to let go of your hurt feelings. You hope Alexis has a nice party. You cheer your teammates on.

You may never know why other people made the choices they did. They may never say they are sorry. Either way, you are free—free of the pinched feeling that hurt and anger bring to your heart.

Looking Through Another's Eyes

People can hurt each other without even knowing or meaning it. Maybe the coach wanted to put Luiz in the game, because he hadn't gotten a chance to play yet. Maybe Alexis didn't invite you because it was a family party.

If someone bothers you or hurts you, it's okay to let them know how you feel—in a kind and calm way.

The other person might explain why she did what she did. This gives you the chance to look at things through her eyes. Different people can see the same things very differently.

Feelings Come and Go

You know you have the power to forgive. You can also choose not to be hurt in the first place. Elena could pout because her brother won't play catch with her. But she decides to find someone else to play with her.

Do you remember a time when you wanted something so much you ached inside? Today, it doesn't matter as much, does it? It's good to know how you feel. It's great to know that many feelings go away. Some come and go very fast.

Your happiness comes from inside your heart. Many times, you can just let sad or mad feelings fly by you. You don't have to hang onto them.

When Others Are Unkind

Forgiving doesn't mean you won't ever get hurt. Just as you can't stop the rain from falling, you can't keep from being hurt sometimes.

When someone hurts you, think before you do anything else. Ask yourself: Where does it hurt? Why does it hurt? How much does it hurt? Often, like the rain, it's only a sprinkle. You know you'll be fine soon.

If it hurts a lot, you need to do something. Tell the other person to stop. If he doesn't stop, then leave. Ask someone bigger and wiser for help. Don't spend time with people who hurt you. You can be forgiving—and still walk away.

Wise People Teach Forgiveness

Some kids think you always need to act "tough" to be strong. But forgiving shows real strength.

Many people all over the world honor the words and example of Jesus. He taught his friends to forgive other people just as they want to be forgiven. Jesus was so strong that he even forgave the people who killed him.

Nelson Mandela was in prison in Africa for twenty-seven years. When he got out, his friends waited for him to get even with the people who had locked him in jail. He said it is better to forgive and to be at peace. He became the leader of his country.

When You Make a Mistake

What if *you* are the one who messed up and needs to be forgiven?

Sometimes, people will tell you to say, "I'm sorry." You've probably said it at times when you didn't mean it yet. It's okay to say it anyway, because your mind and heart can catch up later. But you have the power to say it and mean it at the very same time. You are not giving in or giving up—you are giving love.

Practice saying words like: "I'm sorry." "I didn't mean to and I hope you're okay." "Excuse me." "Forgive me." These are words of love. When you use them, love will come back to you.

Forgive Yourself

Admitting a mistake is hard. We like to be right. But no one gets it right all the time. Look at how hard a baseball pitcher tries to throw three strikes—and how often he doesn't succeed. But he tries again the next inning.

Give yourself a new inning. A mistake is not a failure. It is simply a chance to try again.

Think about all the things you do well every day. Maybe you helped set the table without being asked. Or you were nice to the new kid at the bus stop.

There may be some things you will never do very well. Mistakes and mess-ups help you decide what to skip and what to keep in your life.

Living in a Forgiving World

There are places in the world where nobody will be the first to forgive. And so the people keep fighting with each other.

The world is made of nations. Nations are made of states. States are made of counties and cities, which are made of neighborhoods. And neighborhoods are made of neighbors—people like you.

When you forgive, you bring peace to your heart and to those around you. If everyone in every neighborhood everywhere would be forgiving, we could put an end to fighting and war. Forgive...and help bring peace to the world!

Carol Ann Morrow is the editor of *Youth Update*, a publication of St. Anthony Messenger Press. She is the author of the booklet *Talking With Your Teens About Prayer and Meditation* and has also written several Elf-help Books for adults. She and her husband live in Cincinnati, Ohio. Her eight-year-old neighbor, Ryan Madsen, shared his experience and understanding of forgiveness, which helped and encouraged her to write this book.

R. W. Alley is the illustrator for the popular Abbey Press adult series of Elf-help books, as well as an illustrator and writer of children's books. He lives in Barrington, Rhode Island, with his wife, daughter, and son. See a wide variety of his works at: www.rwalley.com.